## Epilogue/Summary

Taquan Jones married Sara Mitchell for better or for worse and they live what seem to be an ordinary life. Taquan and Tyron Jones have always done what they were supposed to do in fulfilling their purpose and becoming the best Politian's' ever. They were ministered to and trained as political officials since birth. To lead the transition of the transformation that was to take place in a society built on transgression and the brutality of wicket works. Who wins the world was never the question. "How?" Is what was always troubling the mind of the trouble makers but, only time will tell that aspect. It wasn't something that can be told but revealed in the process.

*"Vengeance is mines said the Lord."*

And again in:

*"Nobody should know the day nor the hour of the coming of the Lord but the Father."*

1

In reading this Urban Action Series of a new world in a world clasping you will be blowing away and left anticipating the visual TV show. This T.V series special, written as a book first, begin the introduction of a story line where lives meet and souls are driven and truly inspired by the will of the most high. They will stop at nothing and there is nothing they won't do in order to see the decree established.

# When God Say Yes.......
## It's only the beginning

# Episode 1

# Sara (Scene 1)

Me and my husband Taquan have been married for one year and we recently moved into our new home down in Savanna, Georgia together. We were looking forward to the day we filled our home with some cute little kids. But, for now we had each other and were content and enjoyed decorating this 4 bedrooms, 2 bathrooms, a full backyard with a pool, a full back deck, front yard, and a drive up two car garage home. It was our dream home that we worked so hard for straight out of college for almost 10 yrs. We purchased our home below market value with homes in foreclosure since the 2008 recession had hit the U.S. We had no mortgage paying the house off in full, allowing us to live comfortably, while building up our non-for-profit organization here in the south.

Back in our home town of New York City, where we had both been raised as kids and where we met as adults. I held an executive position at a high-end advertising company for small businesses straight out of grad school. Before, we relocated here in Atlanta I was at the peak of my profession as a Specialized Advertiser: who redeveloped companies' infrastructure so that they could get a bigger return on investment. It was remarkable how I and my team worked, especially when launching a campaign.

The company (TURF.inc) CEO Jeff offered me the chance to open an office down in the south with double pay, full benefits, and any other accommodation I wanted. I told him how much I appreciated the offer and would consider but was interested in launching a non-profit organization and that needed my time and attention. As well as, spending time with my husband. I wanted kids. I'm 30 and the clock was ticking. Not that I told my ex-boss that last part but, he got the point. Especially when he asked "how long is the honey moon going to be?" I said one full year besides our 2 weeks' trip. We had a laugh at that but, I wash serious. I am going to enjoy this year coming, I remember thinking to myself.

The company gave us a $100,000 as a donation to our not-for-profit and told me the contract will be waiting if I consider his offer. I couldn't thank them enough and knew in the future that may be a good idea to sign the contract for a south office. Either way it would help our NPO community to exile by creating jobs which was the plan.

My husband's high academic performance in Computer Science had him pinned for by top private companies even while he studied. Upon graduation he accepted a local job as a computer analysis at a huge company in New York. Within 5 yrs. something changed and he became more secretive as to what exactly his occupation was. I wasn't any fool and explained that to him verbally telling him, his secrecy had caused me to do some investigating. I could only find out that the company was a protected government agency with little to no information in regards to what the company actually do professionally.

The funny thing is my computer had been acting weird since researching the company and he still hasn't gotten around to fixing it. Smh (Shaking my head).

I remembered the first time months went by, like 2 months, and I hadn't heard from him nor could I contract him. The shit scared me half to death I was frantic praying he was ok. I repeatedly called police who finally told me that filing a report wasn't necessary and he would contact me soon. After cursing them out and threating to sue them. I finally got myself to calm down enough to realize that they knew something but weren't telling me and there was nothing I could do, but wait.

It had been the longest time he had ever stayed away, as he did take trips from time to time, but not ever for this length of time. The longest ever was two weeks at a time and we were usually overseas. Do to my occupation as an advertiser I traveled and took frequent trips as well. But, most of the time I took a trip it was because Taquan was barely home. If it wasn't the long hours working it was the frequent out-of-nowhere-just-started-happening trips for both of us. No one seemed to be home lately at all. When I would get home at times there would be a note or signs indicating I just missed him being there.

I was coming back to our place just how I left it, with just me alone and that started to bother me. So I started planning our wedding he was mines in that I was confident in. Him cheating hadn't ever crossed my mind. Taquan love was for me and me alone like the heavenly father himself strictly made this man for me. Like, Adam and Eve.

My plans were the wedding first as we both wanted it in our hometown something simple, fun, and memorable. We had long decided on relocating to Atlanta once we had our wedding and had just finished paying off our house, so relocating was second. The third was developing and launching our not-for-profit organization. While of cause, we would be working on creating our inheritors. He was all for it. But, for some reason I felt like I was missing something when it came to my husband, like something he wasn't saying was taking place in his life.

I just brushed it off. I just wanted to spend my life with my husband in peace, not in this fast paste and glamourous working environment. Corporate life isn't appealing after a while but, it is when you fresh out of college excited to be making big bucks. We had more than enough in our joint account to live off of comfortably. There was no telling what was in his personal account I knew he had. Mines held almost a hundred grand Ijs (I'm just saying).

Once we moved into our house I thought things would change but they didn't. The more I spoke about us reconnecting and spending more time together. The more he would shower me with gifts and romance me till I stopped talking about it. I played sick for a whole month one time and he stayed right by my side as much as he could till duties he so kept secret could not be put off any longer. He was here with me one minute and gone the next leaving me angry, disappointed, and bothered. But, my love never withering for my husband it did the opposite and just grew fonder of him. I just cherished some of our best memories in my heart for ramification moments. Love was an understatement I was in love that was renewed every day that we were blessed to see another day. I never knew a love like this before my husband, that made you want to tell the world "I'm in Love" and wouldn't change it for nothing in the world.

I looked around after he left this morning and felt so anger that we barely spent our full year together after our marriage as we had agreed. I won't bring a kid into this type of environment with him barely being home, I need him here. I thought to myself. Feeling frustrated I grabbed my jacket and left the house to get some air needing the opportunity to think clearly. The way I was feeling a drink was much needed a double shot of henny on the rocks. But, instead I settled for something more subtle and proactive.

We have been here 8 months at this point and I wanted to see the town. We started visiting a few spots and land marks but haven't had time to see anything more. I jumped in my car and pulled off. You want to know about the people living in a town, visit their Mall; you bound to see firsthand the attitudes they convey. The mall was in town as we lived outside the town in a suburban area where the homes where spread out given you more acreage.

I had been in the Mall shopping for 2 hours when I decided to grab a bite to eat. So I decided to check out the food and settled on Thai chinses fast food choice in the food court. The food court choices included a Soul food Pam's kitchen, Chicken and waffles, McDonalds, Checkers, and Fresh direct salad bar. After I received my food I walked to the courts eating area where tables and chairs were arranged in two seaters, four seaters, and six seaters in a large area. I spotted a four seater as all the two seaters seemed to be taken. The table was clean of food remains from a prior customer, so I sat and laid my food out after placing my bags down.

I had made purchases at Guess, Nike, Polo, North Face, and Urban Outfitters shops. Please don't think I purchased this for me or my husband. We wear nothing but causal clothing as we continually, in every aspect of our public appearance, wanted to advocate the good of our cultural communities.

I have been in the lime light a lot as I turned companies' with large debt around to making huge profits, top companies in their prospective market. Taquan made frequent public appearances since college speaking in front of large gathering about this social issue or another. So appearance was everything to us in representing who we are.

The purchases were presents for the kids expected to arrive to their new permanent home Jones Lil Village our non-for-profit home. The kids arriving will remain here as foster kids unless; a permanent home within their families became available, they go away to college on scholarships, they're discharged because of behavioral reasons (a last result), or they leave.

The group-home was opening in a few weeks right before Christmas; we planned to have a Christmas party for the staff and residents. She loved the architecture design that made their dream a reality they had did extraordinary work. The house had been fully equipped to meet the needs of all the children who would live there. There were 4 full bathrooms; 2 for boys and 2 for girls on the two top floors, one for each on each floor. There were 10 bedrooms; 6 of the rooms were for the older kids, 2 sharing per room, with 2 college dorm beds and two desktop computers in each of the 6 rooms located on the 3$^{rd}$ floor. The 4 young kids' rooms; 2 for only girls and 2 for only boys held 6 kids in each room. Each of the young kids rooms had been designed so that each of the four rooms connected to the activity room filled with games, toys, T.V's, and everything else imaginable for them to enjoy. There was a room on each side of the activity room and two at the back. There was a Library room and resource room with computer print and fax machine and other learning tools. They had a secure pool that needed adult access for all ages, a mini park and basketball court in the backyard.

The dinner area was connected to the kitchen area in the back of the house on the 1st floor. There were round tables and chairs grouped as four sitters shattered orderly, and vending machines. The security desk was in the front by the entrance and anybody entering will have to be buzzed in upon verification. The staff area and their offices was behind the security office, as nobody could enter the building without going through them first.

Taquan was very strict about the security of the location; you couldn't enter without getting though the gate security and no access to the back yard without first entering the house. There were cameras everywhere besides the bathrooms and bedrooms for law reasons. Besides tight security the place was remarkable. We designed the inside in comfortable home accessories and decided to let the staff and children design there spaces to show who they were, limitation of course to no weird shit.

Scheduled first would be the Open house event of "Liberty House foundation" fund raising to welcome "Jones Lil Village" NPO into the NPO community in the south. This will be the introduction of our mission and vision presented to others who shared similar goals dedicated to the community. I was proud of how everything turned out and was looking forward to expanding and opening other locations, and, to include families as well.

I really did feel honorable and satisfied in our accomplishments me and my husband hard work and focus really paid off. I wasn't only happy at our accomplishments for us but sharing, encouraging and helping others was the most satisfying.

"Hi." Someone said breaking my chain of thought.

I looked up to see a women standing there with a tray of food in her hands and a few bags on her arm looking at me. She smiled and continued.

"There aren't any more seats left and I had ordered my food to stay. Do you mind?" She gestured towards the empty chairs at my table.

I moved my soda and tissues more in front of me to show that space won't work; I looked at my pocketbook in the seat next to me and left it there. The seat that was diagonally across from me was left available which was about right. Atlanta was a great city and place to live with its beautiful landscapes. Atlanta had upbeat citizens with a strong temple you felt it resonated all the way from Alabama. It's just some real weird mixing of gender Atlanta has a very large LGTB community here and transgender laws had recently be changed causing problems.

I wanted to play it cool and not jump into nothing not even making acquaintances till that settled.

"Sure." I said Looking at the seat diagonally across from me. Just to make sure she got the message. Excuse my passiveness but chalk it up to cautiousness in a new city. After seating her belonging and food down she stuck out her hand. I looked up; I think she remembered some logic.

"Yea. You probably wouldn't want to shake a stranger hand while you are eating. Where is my manners' right?-"

"I'm Tameka by the way. Thanks again." She said.

I said nothing as I finished chewing the food that was in my mouth. "Nice to meet you." I finally said as I returned to eating.

"You not from here are you? Sounds like you from up North."

I have heard that so much I should probably where something that read "My accent is not going nowhere" if that what they thought it was before I stand out and hear that forever.

"Yup. That I am." I said flatly.

"Are all you guys from New York this unfriendly." She chuckled.

"Probably not you should visit one day and find out."

I closed my empty container of food. Finished drinking my juice then grabbed my things to go. Double checking to make sure I had everything, I proceeded to leave. When I glanced her way this Tameka chick was stirring at me, I felt uneasy and barely knew who this chick was.

"Have a nice day." I said and walked away not waiting to hear a reply.

When I left the food court I decided to take my time. I wanted to see the other shops that I missed like Victoria Secret, I might grab something sexy for tonight. Shopping had already lightened up my mood I was even thinking about cooking dinner tonight. I browsed a few jewelry shops then I stopped in Victoria Secret and couldn't resist buying something. I grabbed, from a small bakery, a fruit cake for desert tonight. I was cooking a dinner and wanted it special. As I was heading to the parking lot I had seen an area over to the right of the entrance. The two overhead signs pointing in that direction showed the bathroom signs for men and women and a sign that read "Trina's Hair, Make-up and Nails". I definitely had to check this out after using the bathroom first.

I want to the bathroom handled my business and came back out a little excited about maybe getting some pampering done, it has been a minute, I've been keeping up with it my appearance myself.

OMGGGGG (oh my Gosh)…….. Were the only words that I can formulate for the screen before my eyes. It looked like something straight out of a magazine. I lie to you not. Tan wood gain furniture, purple and white was the color of the decor in the interior design. The place felt gigantic as I walked through the automatic doors. So much going on you seen an area for nails to the left, make-up looked like it was in the back and hair was being done to the right of the entrance large space. The soft music playing in the background had a relax your soul feeling. A receptionist was seating behind a huge desk and greeted me as I walked in.

"Good afternoon ma'am."

I had a big smile on my face looking around as I walked up to the desk.

"This is amazing." I said. Just walking into the place you felt clic and fashionable.

The receptionist was now standing, she smiled back looking friendly and professional dressed in the company's purple and gold salon uniform. Matching the décor of the salon the colors went well together.

I approached the desk and shook my head. The place had an expensive and elaborate feel to it and things seemed to have a flow going.

" Does Trina the music artist own this?" I couldn't help but ask her.

"Yes she does ma'am." She talked so politely the south really had manners you rarely seen back in my hometown.

"Is this your first time here?" She asked me.

"Yes Sweetie. But it won't be my last if the service is as good as the place looks."

"We offer Beauty services on the first floor and Spa treatment on the second floor. Will you like to get a service today?"

"Yup." I said it was going down tonight baby, mama was popping out.

"I am Dominique your hostess this afternoon. I will need to open you a tab using a debit or credit card?"

"Sure." I said pulling out my wallet to give the young lady a credit card.

"Thank you."

She typed the information into a computer off my card. I got a chance to look around at the chandeliers hanging beautifully, the professional service being offered, the flat screen TV's around, and a nice lounge area and the commodities. She passed me back my card and an iPad. Wait. I get an IPad just for getting service done here was the expression on my face.

"Welcome Mrs. Jones. To "Trina Salon Palace" may you have a pleasurable first time experience here at Trina's we are honored to service you. Enjoy."

I was still confused about this IPad. "And this little device is for?"

"Welllllllll."

I heard someone say behind me and turned around to see who it was. Tameka. O.K. we was about to fight she interrupting my me time a little too much. I was starting to feel like she was looking for a friend and right now I really wasn't looking for one.

"The IPad let you know what services we offer, who is performing the services and what your wait/time for the service(s). Also, it tells you under my bill icon how much the services are costing you minus the commodities which is free. And-" She said adding. "It buzzes every time you switch a service."

Interesting but what was complexing was why was she telling me. I steered at her, really not wanting to be rude. I was nodding my head the way New Yorkers do when they say "yeah...yeah'.

"Here is my card." She said laying a card on the iPad. "I work in the massage parlor upstairs on the second level if you ever get time." And she walked off.

A young man said right this way ma'am regaining my focus as he offered me a drink. Damn can this get any better? I ordered a glass of wine as he guided me to the shampoo station and said he would be right back with my drink. A shampoo girl introduced herself and prepped me for a wash.

On the IPad with the help of the shampoo girl and the sever I ordered; a wash and set with a deep condition and blow dry and flat iron. After washing my hair and applying the deep condition a shower cap was placed on my head for 15 minute under the drier. As I sat down my drink was severed to me. I swear I was content in my life and knew this was a privilege and pleasure I didn't take for granted. When you blessed, and know it, you aren't

stressed. Cheers to that.

# Taquan (Scene 2)...............

*"At this stage of the operation I am the head of the operation the executor in a plan that won't be stopped by any enforcers. No matter the force they so dangerously try to enforce. How can they ever think they could win a battle that wasn't theirs in the first place? Unknown reckless minded people who only quests are destruction and mayhem throughout the world. Their time in high places has ended. Made Man don't fall. For "He became the chief corner stone" shows our brother lives. What we needed has been given and what has been given cannot be taken away. Your evil pilot was destroyed in one day in two it fail in three behold there it was no more. What have been destroyed we will speak of no more for it has passed and behold the time is new. Sustain you have sustained it you proclaimed it throughout Israel and whispered it in the ear of Juda. I AM' I AM Ohhhh' I AM'. Listening they did not and had a heartening of their hearts. Oh Stubborn people with stiff necks how stubborn of you. Passing such*

*vulnerability down generation to generation unyielding in*

*ignorance to destroy who it consumed. Oh great ones of old*

*how your shepherds have little faith and blow toward the*

*way strong winds beat."*


**Ring…. Ring…Ring**

I had to shake the sleep off as I came awake to a phone

ringing. I must of does off, something that was starting to

happen a lot lately.

"Hello" I said barely registering the name that appeared on

the screen of my cell phone.

"Where you at?" the caller asked me sounding real hurried

on the phone.

"I'm in my office I believe." I looked around as I was still

shaking off the sleepiness I was feeling, my mind was a

little puzzled as well.

"Yeah man. I'm in my office." I was a little confused as to

where I was till I looked around. I rubbed my hand across

my face than rubbed my eyes.

"I'm heading to you now bruh" Click...... The caller hung up.

**15 minutes later..........**

"Hey man. What's up?" Tyron said walking in my office.

"I'm looking over these reports and press releases. What's good with you?" I said.

Tyron shook his head with a smirk on his face. "Since I woke you up huh? I know you were napping again. What's up with that?"

"I was and I am not sure. Started a few weeks ago someone be talking to me it feels like I'm being ministered to when I nap off like that."

Tyron was laughing now. "You sure Sara is not pregnant?"

"So what if she is?" I said looking at him like he had four heads not understanding what was so funny.

"I'm not quite sure that's the end of it."- "So what if she is?" He said mimicking after me.

"You have quite a lot going on here bruh with this campaign coming up and she not knowing all these years, what your occupation really is. You're a top government official who has been with a woman 10 years who still thinks you're a Computer Analyst. I think you clearly have some ethical soul searching to do when it comes to clearing the conscience."

Tyron started laughing harder now. I hated his laughing fits.

"Are you serious right now? You really said all of that in one sentence like you care. When the last time you even had a woman?" Taquan found nothing funny. What was he here for anyway it sounded urgent on the phone? Perhaps that's what they needed to discuss. Not his wife.

"Having a woman is different than getting pussy. I get pussy but, I have decided I'm a chill recently so that's what you have noticed. I'm getting too old for the bullshit I've decided." He seemed serious enough saying that.

"Nice." I said being real sarcastic he was blowing mines.

"But, there is something so unethical going on with you right now I can feel it." He continued to say.

"So what sounded so urgent?" I said changing the subject.

"We might have trouble arriving." Tyron said looking serious all laughter gone from his face.

"I am not sure who this group is or if they connected to someone here in the states. They have been coming and going the last couple of months and they're activities are spacious. The group arrived last night in the middle of the night coming through from the outskirts of the North American Ocean over by the Bahamas direction, according to reports, from Cuba cargo to the States."

In the mist of Tyron speaking he handed me the folder he was holding in his hand. Inside the folder were reports and pictures of the same trio in most of the pictures. I looked over everything with a quick eye the pictures repeatedly had the same three guys even though you can tell the pictures had been token at different times. The picture contents showed the trio mingling with different people; it looked like business as usual of some sort.

The background of the pictures is what really caught my eye it had the boarder gates visual. People aren't allowed to move around with liberty in those areas they're very restricted areas. So whatever it is they were negotiating should not have been, being done there. I find this potentially a problem on more levels then one. One thing for sure that the individuals in the photos were from foreign countries. Who have no respect for law enforcement, two; US have no problem going to war. Whatever they were negotiating is not the nature of business that goes on, on that end or part of town.

"No one really knows that their forming there but as being we surveillance the boarders closely for activities of any kind our team noticed it. So far we know they came with export to foreign good manufacturing plant on the out skirts of Florida. To then be shipped to Hawaii for further shipping for the families on the boarders of Puerto Rico for the immigrating Haitians."

He paused as we both understood the value in that humanitarian value.

"Observation shows the TriO changes frequencies of strategy and don't always follow the procedure causing a few problems with the boarder personals. The people they meet at the boarders come in on the ships when they come in. Hard to get fast and current information when they aren't yet all electronically equipped overseas. And given the nature of what they're coming for, Aid for those families." Tyrone added.

He had stop speaking and I seat going over everything I learned about the case.

"I am officially opening an investigation into the case documented under alias TriO." I was writing note on the folder to put in the data system.

"Our team has the highest number of watch points at the boarder lines. Even with the new hiring do we still process that?" I asked him as I picked up the report I was going over earlier.

I believe it contained the information I was asking for. I recently had one of my many trips out of the country and had just got back a few days ago.

"Yes but I did do some research still within the department to see if any other units reported any sightings. There was a report or two of disorderly conduct and a head official agent did visit the deport owner of the operation who donate the food. Who lives in another country. Citation was given; an official warning of restricted activities or injunction of penalty if the matter was to not improve in regulation of guidelines. Was the only order on record."

"Give me everything you have email it to me. I will review it and give you my official opinion of what will happen regarding the matter. Continue close surveillance. Are there any other important matters I should be briefed about?"

Between me getting married and traveling for this pre-campaign and appearances overseas. I feel uninformed of what is happening right under my nose. Could be overwhelming at times.

"You have a mission and this interruption of things is the least of our problems anything worth knowing you will know bruh." He was right about that.

"I will finish up here and look over this information including what you will send me. Are you going to be at the office today?" I asked him.

"Nah I need to make a few runs."

I gave him that look I always give him when he says that statement. Wasn't about nothing he knew exactly where I stood, what make you can also break you.

"Copy." I stood up from behind my desk and gave my little brother a pound as we said our usual salute.

"He lives."

"He lives." Tyron replied then turned and left my office.

When Tyron left the office I was in deep thought. Situations like this were always the case, not mattering, the million ways the state tried to deal with the problem at the boarders. Tariff laws weren't easy to deal with. Countries build things and make it available to the people in their country which also makes it exclusive at time making it of value. When other country man can freely come and visit and/or enter of free will, they can leave with your hard earned valuable inventions. Taxes are also important for the land and for the product to exchange hands, for these reasons alone policies and regulation are put in place. Policies in place were revised to restrict even more the limits of imports per year after the recession. Recently the agency moved seasoned officials of lower ranks, who were looking to advance to a higher level, to new positions at the borderlines. My team had trained the men and women to fill the positions; my team was the site mandating officials who approve clearance of all import and export coming in and leaving this port. The new hires on site overseen smaller divisions and check point.

My government official position played only a small part in the mission I was here to perform. I knew the mission was about to unfold in its darkest moments and the circumstance are like no other. The naps had to be the anxiety attacks my superior told me would come at some point because of the duress my body would experience; as a transformation would happen inside of me spontaneously. I would stick to the plan no matter what happens, no buts and no ands about it. This is where all the training and hard work we endured for the decree to take place will soon be in effect and it will all be over. Only then will we be able to live normal lives and not just look like we living normal lives.

Tonight I had decided to go home early I missed spending time with my wife plus, this TriO case had been on my mind all day. The closer we got to the inside voting of who will run for president both democrats and republicans will be nominated up and reviewed by the state for requirements and qualification before announcing runners up. My presidential seat was a ticket to me as part of my mission all I had to do was follow the steps which had been laid out before me since birth. But, the closer we got the more I felt things won't be the same on the other side. Not sure if that was a god or bad feeling. So Tyron was probably right talking to my wife at this point probably wasn't such a bad idea.

As I pulled into the garage I noticed the house looked quiet too quiet I still had to get use to this country life. I walked in the house and closed the door behind me locking it. Something smelled good. Damn good. I put my briefcase down by the door and started following the smell; I loosened my tie and pulled my shirt out of my pants as I headed to the kitchen. Walking into the kitchen I walked into what men would consider a very delightful, appealing, and the most inviting way to be greeted by the women you love. Sara was binding over taking something out the oven. My groin got hard instantly I leaned against the doorway of the kitchen, she hadn't noticed me yet.

I watched her check a pan and then leaned up and place the pan on the counter. My eyes want down to her ass which was seating right do to the 4-inch stiletto red heels she was wearing. Her legs looked as smooth and inviting as my eyes did its roaming. The sexy lingerie she was wearing in white and red, similar to a maids outfit in design but was too sexy for any maid to be parading around in was lit. Her hair was flowing down her back and he could tell it had been freshly done. She swung it over her shoulder and finally noticed me there.

For a few seconds I felt like I was hypnotized by her. My wife was beautiful and I felt like the luckiest man in the world right then and there. She smiled noticing me watching her and I know seen the lust that must be vibrating strongly from me. She turned fully around facing me. I felt my heart leap in my chest and I wanted to pour my love into her. I slipped my hands in my pocket and slowly moved towards her. I smelt her sweet perfume before I could reach her it heightened my hormones. I touched the side of her face with one hand, our lips touched and she pulled me closer. Why did she do that we won't be eating any dinner no time soon.

I picked my wife up as we continued to kiss passionately. I didn't realize I missed her so much till now. I pulled back to make sure we made it to the living without falling as I left the kitchen carrying her. Sara continued to trail kisses down my neck while her hands were unbuttoning my shirt. As we reached the couch and I laid her down my lips returned to hers. She moaned as I grabbed her legs to position her under me. There was too much clothes between us and I stood up to take off everything as I watch her undo her lingerie. I moved between her legs on the couch and watched the lust in her eyes as my hands messaged her thighs, to that special place between her legs. As my finger enters her she moaned and closed her eyes.

I was trying hard to not rush things she wanted a special night apparently I wouldn't want to spoil it. I teased and played with her before replacing my finger with my tough. As I sucked and licked till I was full off her juices, she called my name and cried her love as she reached the bleak of cumming. Her body jerked as she released her loving and I finally released my grip on her. I started trailing kisses up her belly to the center of her breast kissing one then the other. She regained herself and wrapped her legs around me as she pushed herself up rolling over and placing me under her. She rubbed against me wetting my groin with her juices she was ready for another go. She rubbed my body as she made her way south I was hard as a rock. Her mouth was warm and damn near undone me. I tried my best to hold it down but her mouth was insulting me. I couldn't take no more and pulled her up to me wanting to feel those lips on my own. She positions me to enter her and I gave a hard push as our mouths touched and explored each other's. I felt and heard her mourn against my mouth as she did, then she started moving up and down slowly.

A few seconds passed and her tempo picked up, as she increased her paste she sat up slowly and continued riding me. I grabbed her hips for support and tried slowing her down but she seemed too increase. It was like heaven as I burst the must fulfilling human pleasure as I groaned like only a man could in a time of such passion. It was then we became one united together in the true nature of husband and wife. With me still into her secret crevice she laid down on my chest seeming to fall asleep immediately. I laid there thinking about what life had in store for us.

I knew telling my wife would feel like betrayal for anyone looking in but, I believed in people ability to handle things better when they knew less. Telling her would only prompt her to ask more questions and I reveal more than I was willing to. She knows about my parents but not what they actually did for a living and how I actually got to where I'm at now.

Don't get me wrong my wife knows me and who I am and in that she can be comfortable, it just wasn't as simple as I made it seem to her. I wasn't just some kid from New York who was lucky enough to make it out. I actually never lived in the hood growing up yes I was from a city but lived in a house in the outer suburbs of NYC towards Albany. As I could remember my parents always had money and I and my brother wanted for nothing. That was another issue who she thought was just a best friend…. Tyrone was my biological blood brother just raised different.

Things in my life had gotten complicated over the years as my rank in politics had been changed 3 times. My wife ability to understand my obligations would come at its own time, based on her own level of understanding and her believe system. I know morality mirrored my own believes and values but people change and I have been distant with her. But in my gut feelings I knew she would handle this situation well and adjust to what has to be done.

How long would that take was depending on her. I would be there every step of the way to make her transition into another life easier. I wouldn't ever leave her nor forsake her she was, is, and will always be. Mines.

As I looked down at my wife sleeping I knew she could handle anything, she was strong and I wouldn't intentional hurt her. The situation itself was out of our hands and had to be no matter the perception of others or theirs, on what life is suppose to be. I eased out of her softness and got up to carry her to our bedroom. She has definitely put on a few pounds word. After placing her in our bed I kissed her and headed to the shower.

A man's job is rarely done. I grabbed my rube and returned down stairs to put the food away and blow out the candles in the dining room. I noticed the bottle of henny on the table in front of the couch in a bucket of ice and decided to have a shot. Been a minute since I had a drink as its usually not my custom to drink, I was definitely making an exception tonight. Tonight was going to be a long one I headed to my home office and powered up my Mac.

# Tyrone (Scene 3 Late that Day).......

"My money" Tyrone said holding his hand out his car window for the money to be placed in his hand by the guy standing there.

"Here." Tuck said placing almost a hundred grand in Tyrone's hand. "You have been acting strange lately what's going on with you?" Tuck looked at me as if expecting a response.

"Man your shit is under your car, just do what you do and I will do what I do, if you want to continue getting this money." I set up in my car indicating I was ready for him to go so I could go.

Tuck shook his head and backed away from Tyron car. Tyrone pulled off before Tuck could say another word.

Just a few more pickups and I will be done. I couldn't wait to get home and chill out. One thing I hated more than being in the streets was that police was watching him closely lately. Over the years I hadn't ever grown accustomed to racial profiling and the prejudice in the system when it came to justification. Whoever was behind the cops watching me was doing a good job at hiding. I had spoken to some people who could get him answers and only knew somebody high up wanted him done. Founding out who that somebody was, was only a matter of time and that was for sure. Till then I would just play it cool you couldn't touch me and that was another fact for sure. I pretty much figured why because they probably thought they knew what I was doing, how totally wrong they would be.

Tuck and Keith was my boys but all my business wasn't their business. I didn't like the fact that if things want down he had co-defendants. Especially ones that never took the time to understand what it was they were doing, there was nothing illegal about it, if ever caught they would be questioned about who I am, without talking they will be out on immunity in 72 hours and keep every dime they ever made. Fast money and what they think I represented because of the undercover position I had since a kid blinded them to finding out the facts about me.

Taquan is biologically my blood brother same mother and father, being ordained and here for a season and a purpose we had been divided once we entered grade school. Everything had been told and ministered to us since birth and we knew before we could talk the nature of our existence. Knowing this still didn't lessen the hurt of losing what felt like my whole life at once. We had been observed since birth to understand better the persons we were to become. Taquan was to be head and I was to be his prodigy. He was the thinking and executor and I was the moving warrior the bodier of the unjust which was accurate description of our personalities.

While his purpose put him in the politically correct socialites I unfortunately had to be in the opposite. He went to the best school lived in our grand mini mansion with a nanny and had all the privileges. I had to live in the hood attend the worse schools and lived a low socialite life even though it was the best of the low private schools, condo, and appeal. It was still located in a diversity dense urban community. Our division was in regards to the world being divided by good and bad we were to understand and represent both.

## Boom…..Boom….. Boom (Scene 4 the Next Morning)

"What the fuck"…… as I woke up I realized the banging was coming from down stairs someone was at my door. I got up and grabbed my gun on the floor by my bed before heading to see who it was this early. With the gun behind my back I grabbed opened the door. "Tameka." I wasn't pleased.

"Good morning Tyron." She said smiling as always.

" I saw your car in the drive way. I thought we could have breakfast since it's been a couple of months since we seen each other." That smile was still on her face.

I was steering at her still tired as hell and wondering why

this chick didn't get it. She was always at my door wanting

to do this are that which was bothering the shit out of me. I

didn't like her like that nor did she seem to be my type.

This bitch always wanted to know something about me, felt

like I was being interviewed around her I did not like that

either. I didn't like that at all. And the funny thing is I

never hit it, considered it once, but never hit it. I was

definitely about to find out why she wasn't heeding my

warnings, serious as I was. I unlocked the screen door, a

home cooked meal sounded good for this talk they were

about to have. I turned to head back upstairs and she went

towards the kitchen being she knew his house so perfectly.

I shook my head.

Since I moved in a few years back Tameka has been

coming around she lived across the way from me. I knew

she would eventually just pop up to my crib it had been a

minute since we spoke. The first time she introduced

herself to me I was in my front yard cleaning up the leafs.

She stopped by saying how she wanted to welcomed me to the neighborhood she said she lived with her grandmother across the street. The house was the brightest yellow I had ever seen and it was the only yellow house on the block and stood out with its many flowers in different colors all around it. A nice size family house overall. I did remember laughing a little when she mentioned it. Which I hoped didn't offend her it was funny in a good way it was an old lady house.

She had gone on to tell me a little history about her growing up there in the neighborhood. She was talking and she noticed my car tags was still NY plates and she knew I wasn't from here. She said she was free the weekend and wouldn't mind showing me around town if I had time. She was cute looked around her early 30's I felt no chemistry or anything, so a tour it was. That didn't mean I hadn't been to Atlanta before and visited its scenes somewhat. Just a native's perspective would be great to view Atlanta through and see what they had to say and saw about life here in Atlanta.

That following Saturday we meet out front with me being the designated driver. She took me first to see a few Historical sites Martin Luther King Jr. historic site, Civil and Human rights center in downtown ATL, visited Buckhead and The King Center the Kings burial center. That night we watched a live Tyler Perry show in the famous fox theater, as one of his shows was in town. That Sunday we visited the famous Tabernacle and Ebenezer churches which were both packed to capacity. After that we hung out from time to time nothing crazy, like I said I wasn't feeling shorty, something about her was keeping this from going any further.

One night I had been out drinking and she called me and said she was struck somewhere and asked me to come pick her up. I sent Taquan who brought her back with him to pick me up I had stayed at the spot we had been chilling at. I had not been ready to leave when she called. Taquan had thought that he would drop us off at home at the same time because she lived across the street. But, when we got to my crib shorty was laid out sleep before Taquan could lay me down.

Taquan said he left leaving me to deal with that, when I finally got around to asking him about it. When I woke up that next morning shorty was lying on top of me kissing my neck and shit. When she realized I was up she tried kissing me in the mouth. I remember her breath smelling like mint which meant she had been up so why hadn't she left. At the time I got so sick to my stomach from the liquor from the night before that her kissing me with that mint taste brought it all up I was pushing her off me and grabbing for the trash bucket by my bed. Caught it just in time or she would have been cleaning up throw up. "What the fuck." I yelled once I was done. "Why the fuck are you in my bed anyway."

She grabbed her stuff and left quickly without saying a word and I was happy for it for this whole situation was nerve racking. I remembered her not coming around for a few weeks and seeing me around the neighborhood was rare as he was always on official business.

She finally popped up weeks later after that incident to my crib unannounced. So I made the decision to fuck her right then and there and send her packing. Since she wasn't getting the picture, one thing he hated was dumb brads. When I answered the door I remember pulling her inside and I started feeling on her body she never stopped me. I pushed her down on my living couch as I had been moving the situation in that direct. This shit wasn't worthy of a bedroom. When she felt back on the crouch she set back up and pulled her shirt over her head. I was standing over the crouch unbuckling my pants when she moved my hand and started to finish the task.

"Stop." I said with so much determination in my voice that she just stared at me. I moved away.

"I really don't want to fuck you shorty. Yeah you pretty, yeah you might really like me, and yeah you may be a good woman for all I know. But none of that shit means anything to me because I'm not feeling you. I would have fucked you just now to just play you. I remember shaking my head feeling sad for shorty the bitch was crazy to be going this strong.

"So you have 2 choices to either stop coming by here. Or I will get a restraining order. Now if I have to get a restraining order you will definite be getting an ass whipping from another female for evening putting me through the bullshit. The call is yours."

She must have thought I was playing to still be sitting in my face right now. He hoped like hell she could fight. She really should think about getting help this situation should not have gone this far. I focused back on the situation.

I had took a shower and dressed in my button up shirt and two piece suit as was my style of dressing since I could remember. I couldn't remember a day in my life that I wasn't told by my foster parents the importance of my appearance and leadership no matter where I was from. I had to learn how to be politically correct even growing up in the hood. I had to still dress and act like my surroundings wasn't my life and at times that was hard. I placed my watch on and a gold chain, small in character, but a 100% gold around my neck. I put on my gold PhD graduate ring, the only ring I have ever worn since receiving it. I glanced in the mirror and was satisfied before heading out and down the stairs. It smelled good.

"Hey." She said without turning around as I walked into the kitchen.

"Smells good." I said as it did. I sat down at a stroll around the kitchen counter. I see she had sat the table but this definitely wasn't one of those calls.

"So what made you stop by my house this morning? I constantly tell you it's unnecessary but since you don't seem to care explain to me why." I said jumping right into the problem.

She turned around after turning the strove off and putting the pot she was holding in her gloved hand back down. Her eyes as she looked at me were saying a million things as they moved around while she formulated the words she wanted to say. I waited.

"I can't help it." She said continuing. "I like seeing you, talking to you, and being around you."

This bitch was fucking impossible she wasn't getting it.

"You do understand I don't like you in that way. And your bullshit makes me uncomfortable."

"Why are you looking at me like that? Why do you seem to hurt me some much and I do nothing but show you love?" She was crying now. I couldn't believe this shit it was time to go.

"Bitch I don't even know you like that we chilled a few times and you know I'm straight forward. Whatever you feeling and want, I am not interested in and really don't care about. I told you your choices you remember that right." She wasn't getting it. Both phone calls had already been made she was at this very second trespassing and didn't know it.

"So you would really have me beat up for falling in love with you Tyron?" She asked me.

"No wrong. I would have you beat up for thinking you can violet my warning even after I asked you nicely."

"Why can't you just accept my gratitude towards you it's not like you have a girl complaining about me coming around or anything?"

"You ready to go. I need to get out of here." I was done with this situation a waste of my fucking time.

"So you are not going to eat your breakfast. I didn't poison it if that's what you thinking."

After today she might wish she had. I told my home-girl to take it easy he just hoped Tameka didn't try fighting back then it was out of both of their control. Self-defense would be used by any means necessary my home girl wasn't going to let no bitch touch her and she was doing me a favor was her words. I waited while she grabbed her bag and jacket. She looked at me hard while I held my front door open. I saw my home-girl car parked in front and knew this problem hard ended harder than necessary. Shorty wasn't respecting my shit as much as I respected females I also knew what they were capable of I witness my man's go through shit I couldn't ever put up with. Females knew how to manipulate a situation to get what they wanted I refused to be a victim to such tactics.

As we walked down the front walk way I turned towards my car. My home-girl got out her car and stood on the side walk. I got in my car and backed out. I gave the two a glance as I did, mainly checking for cars coming as I backed out. I see one punch then another Tameka swung back missing I knew it was a wrap for her than as I pulled off. Some people learn the hard way.

# Tameka (Scene 5)...........

I was sent for a reason but all that changed the day I actually met my target. He was nothing how the many reports I've read described him being. I questioned for the first time the source behind the information obtained. I specially trained for situations like this but seemed so unprepared for the real thing.

Something wasn't adding up and it's not me being blinded by my feelings for the target. Something just isn't adding up. Now I'm limping to my crib because I let someone who is taking boxing lessons punch on me a few times. One move and I could have stopped that bitch from breathing than watched the scared look of death pass across her face as she pleaded for help. Then before a minute was up and she lose too much oxygen to the brain I would have opened her wind pipes and watched her be thankful......
Or I could have just shot the bitch with my 38 that was tucked in my purse.

"Ouch." A pain shot up my side as I sat down on the couch with an ice pouch in my hand. I think I made the chick mad when I swung back, it doesn't feel like a broken rib but definitely a black and blue. She lucky. I would say that much.

Ding Dong…… Ding Dong…………Ding Dong…..

"Who the hell can that be?" I was just about to lay down when the door bell rung. "Ouch" I felt the pains again as I sat back up and stood up to see who was at the door.


Ding Dong …..Ding Dong………

I opened the door to a mail lady standing there with an envelope in her hand and the biggest smile on her face. What the fuck she so happy for I thought to myself.

"Hi may I help you?" What looked to be a mail lady was standing there

"Good evening mam' I have certified mail for a Mrs. Thomas. Is this her address?"

"Yes it is." Thinking it was something for my grandmother.

"Where do I sign for it?" I took the envelope and slipped it under my arm as I reached for the electronic pad in her hands. I signed my name and handed it back to her.

"Are you Tameka Thomas?" The mail lady asked puzzling me by the question.

I just stared at the young girl who looked to be in her late 20's. With the smile still on place on her face she slipped one hand and her pocket and calmly said.

"You have been served." The smile left her face and she turned around heading back down the walk way to a waiting black service car that I hadn't noticed before.

I stared at her back as she turned and walked away could this day get any worse. I closed the door as the car pulled off. I sat back down on the couch forgetting the pain and tore opened the envelope. My assumption was right I am not dealing with a drug cartel this was totally something different and far better fetched. She could only imagine what the truth was and this was only the beginning of her fitting correctly the pieces of the puzzle.

**3 years earlier**...............................

*My first case was given to me by the ambassador in May of 2012. My training for over 20 years was complete and I was an intelligence operator for Cuba. I had been born and raised in Cuba my parent migrated here in the early 1920's during the great depression. I remember very little of my parents who sent me to boarding school back in Cuba by the time I was older enough to attend. I rarely return home for a visit with my parents. Seeing them became absenteeism in my life and when I did visit there were always so many officials around my home occupying their attention. I was always happy to be home and would behavior good for the nanny so they can tell my parents and they would keep me home seeing I wasn't bad. This didn't work before I knew it I was back at boarding school with a long period before returning home again.*

*I knew my parents loved me by their constant visits to the boarding school to observe how I was doing and check on me. They think they were being discreet but most of the time I knew they were there; I was hurt when they did speak to me before leaving. And I had a cell phone since I could remember and would get I love you texts and we would exchange pictures, which my mother and father always did since I left. They would come every year to the school on picture day and take what they called a family photo. The one sentiment I looked forward to, seeing my parents always excited me. I'm not sure if it was because I missed them are because I knew they were somebody important. Mommy always looked good and neat and well put together with quiet demeanor. My pops was handsome and always wear suits his voice was always so cool, he was very protective of me and my mother and told me when I want to high school, that me being at boarding school was the safest place for me to be, giving his profession. I had just turned 14 and knew what professionals meant but profession through me off. "If I can send your mother to boarding school I would" I remember him saying and laughing it off.*

*My second year in high school I got a call from mama saying she had a surprise for me for when I come home in two weeks. I was a nervous wreck by the time the two weeks came and was out the car before the driver can come to a full stop in front of my parents' house.*

*"Mama I remember yelling as I barged into the house and ran right into my father who was heading my way. He grabbed me and hugged me picking my up off my feet.*

*"Hi baby." He said with a warm smile and tinkle in his eyes. "You've gotten taller." He said putting me back down on my feet and holding me by my shoulders to get a good look at me. I was smiling and anxious to see what mommy surprise was.*

*"Where is mom dad she has a surprise for me." The last time I asked for a horse it was a surprise for me when I got*

*home. The next time it had been a dog to keep at school. I*

*hadn't asked for noting this time.*

*'It's been killing me to know dad. Where's mom dad?" I*

*said glancing around for any sign of her.*

*"So daddy gets no love." He said looking hurt. "You know*

*these surprises be from me too?" He said. Taking hold of*

*my hand and leading the way.*

*"I know daddy." I said giving his hand a squeeze. I did*

*know, mommy tell me all the time how much he loved them*

*and we should be grateful to him for what he does for us. I*

*hugged his arm as we reached the top of the spiral stair*

*case we just walked up. As we got closer to my parents'*

*bedroom I heard noises that made me nervous and my*

*hands started to sweat. I looked up at my father who looked*

*down at me.*

*"You that nervous sweet pea?" My father asked me feeling*

*the change in demeanor sounding a little concerned. He let*

*go of my hand and wrapped his arm over my shoulder.*

*"It's not that bad." He said as he slowly pushed opened*

*their bedroom door.*

*Nothing............ No mommy and I didn't see a surprise." I*

*slowed down to give the room a thorough look. There*

*wasn't anything resembling a surprise. My father opened*

*the door to the adjutant room which is my bedroom and*

*waited for me to catch up and walk through the day.*

*I froze in my steps as my room came into my focus there*

*was baby stuff all over my room from where I stood froze I*

*could see pinky on the left side and blue on the right. Did*

*my parents have babies? My father nudged me inside as he*

*softly closed the door. As I moved further into my now old*

*room obviously. I finally saw my mother looking as*

*beautiful as ever holding to babies in her arms as she*

*hymned and rocked softly back and forth. A smile spread*

*across mommy face as she seen me.*

*"Hi princess." she said as my father took one of the babies*

*and she kept one. "Didn't expect a surprise like this did*

*you baby." She must have read the expression on my face.*

*She got up and walked to where I had been standing since I walked in the room.*

*I could only shake my head "no" as she gave me nice warm hug.*

*"I have two new people in our family I will like you to meet. Your twin brother and sister, this is Angela." She said pointing to the baby she was holding and then to the one dad was holding. "And this is Andrew."*

*I didn't know what to say so I just stood there saying nothing. I was confused about how the babies got here I thought I was the only child. These two had some explaining to do. I think my father read my expression. "Sweetie." He said.*

*I did not know if he was talking to mommy are me I looked to him. He was looking at my mother. "I think we got some explaining to do. And you girls need a birds and bees talk. Shall we leave the babies here with the nurse while we have something to eat?"*

*"That sounds fine." My mom looks at me one last time and I noticed a little pain in her eyes. She lay Angela down in the pinky crib. This surprise was definitely the biggest one thus far.""*

As my mind came back into focus the document in my hands was an order of protect to protect the plaintiff Tyrone Jones, against Defendant Tameka Thomas. The order of protection explained what that is meant to include, as well as for how long, and the consequences if it's violated in anyway. I didn't have the right to appeal the judgment, nor did this notice contain a hearing date. Who was Tyrone Jones because he definitely was not a top drug cartel as I had accounting him of being through his observation reports and her surveillance.

Who was Tyrone Jones? And why was I really given this case? It was Time I found out.

So I decided to start with the people I knew to be in his life from my observation reports. His best friend who coincidently had the same last name as him and who resemble him. Also had a restricted portfolio as to who he was and what he did. Upon my researching him there was a government security blockage. I had some people back home trying to find out more information about him. So I focused on the wife of the best friend and had followed her to the mall with plans of befriending her. This task should be easy as people new to a city look for friendly people to help them get to know others.

As we pulled into the parking lot I watched her parked then I parked my care a few feet away and got out. I followed her around as she shopped staying out of view of so she wouldn't notice me in the shadows watching her. After about 2 hours or so she decided to take a break which I took as the prefect opportunity to introduce myself. I grabbed my food and headed to the table where she was seating.

"Hi." I said to get her attention as she was eating with her head down.

She looked up to see me standing there with a tray of food in my hands and a few bags on my arm looking at me. I smiled and continued. "There aren't any more seats left and I had ordered my food to stay. Do you mind?" I gestured towards the table and three empty chairs.

She moved her soda and tissues more in front of her and left her pocketbook in the seat next to her. The seat that was diagonally across from her was the only one left available. Her stand-offish-ness was apparent. "Sure." She said Looking at the seat diagonally across from her.

After setting my belonging and food down I stuck out my hand to test my observation of her. She looked up without reaching to shake my hand as to say do I know. I played it off as if I remembered same logic and manners she probably didn't know where my hands been. She was thinking I guessed.

"Yea. You probably wouldn't want to shake a stranger hand while you are eating. Where is my manners' right? I'm Tameka by the way thanks again." I said.

She said nothing as I finished chewing the food that was in my mouth. "Nice to meet you." She finally said as she returned to eating.

"You not from here are you? Sounds like you from up north."

I bet she heard that a lot since being here.

"Yup. That I am." She said flatly. Not seeming in the mood for socializing.

"Are all you guys from New York this unfriendly." I said at a bad attempt to lighting the atmosphere at the table shit was colder than ice.

"Probably not you should visit one day and find out." She said closing her empty container of food. She finished drinking her juice then grabbed her things to go. I watched her double check to make sure she had everything and proceeded to leave. When she glanced my way I was watching her. I can tell she felt a little uneasy. "Have a nice day." She said and walked away.

I let a few minutes pass before disregarding the rest of my uneaten food and following her. She visited a few my shops as she made her way to the park lot I assumed, before she can exit the mall she notice the Salon Parlor to left of the entrance to the mall as she passed the entrance to check something out I slipped inside the Salon Parlor. She follow suit a few moments later. The hostess greeted her by the door I listen for an opportunity to try and befriend her again.

"Good afternoon mam'. Will you be getting any service done today?" I heard the hostess ask her from my position in the waiting area I pretended to be watching reading a magazine my back was turned to them.

"Yes."

"Ok. I am Dominique I will be your hostess this afternoon. I will need to open you a tab using a debit or credit card first?"

"Sure." She said.

"Thank you." I heard the hostess said.

After a few moments the hostess spoke again. "Welcome

Mrs. Jones to the "Trina Palace" may you have a

pleasurable first time experience here at Trina's. We are at

your pleasure of services. Enjoy."

"Well." I said coming up from behind Sara she turned

around to see who it was and if I was talking to her. I was. I

noticed her looking at the iPad in her hands before turning

around the hostess had yet to explain to her how it work I

took the initiative.

"That." I said pointing to the IPad in her hand. "Let you

know what services we offer, who is performing the

services and your wait time for the service. Also, how

much the services are costing you so you know minus the

commodities and it buzzes every time you switch a

service."

She just stood there stirring at me. She was really making

me start to feel awkward.

"Here is my card." I said laying a card on the iPad in her hand. "I work in the massage parlor upstairs on the second floor if you ever get time." And I walked off.

She knew it couldn't be her and was really starting to assume people from New York had attitude problems. First Tyron attitude and now Sara's there was a pattern happening here a trend. I assumed their secretive life style put them in a position to be stand offish not knowing who to trust. Barriers humans put up to keep others from getting close were my area of specialty. I was trained to breakdown and enter by learning, adapting, and slowing gaining access to what they was hidden inside.

Valuable information put in the right hands to outside sources could do societies they systemize ultimate reign. Not to say it would be easy no matter how hard and long I and ours have trained for the perspectives. These man were man of renew with interiors that couldn't be broken nor destinies destroyed. My people thought through their heart were the only way in and several females had been trained expertly in knowing how and implementing those concepts. In ways to open the heart of a male while he lets his guards down and grows more vulnerable around you.

This was amazing to me that my first case was my worst case scenario. I couldn't have that happening as there was a multitude of things on the line with what the infiltrations of Mr. Tyron Jones. He was pissing a lot of people off and what could happen as oppose to that was more terrifying then anything. Either I get to bottom of what was really going on here and make a final call or it can all blow over taking down a lot of people with it. Like me. The agency in Cuba could send another Op in to compromise the mission and I could be left in the dark to not interfere with the operation. Causing confusion and unintentional interference of missions, things were about to blow over when it was all said and done, I could feel it.

I cannot figure out where I went wrong with Tyron as we started good hanging out and vibing. I felt him pull back and I accounted it to him catching feelings for me and not knowing how to express them. So I decided to make myself more available to him to draw him in and express to him the feelings were neutral. That shit seemed to piss him off and things seemed to go downhill from there between us. I decide I would give him space and let him think it over or just let the negative effects blow over.

My mission was on the line. Still I got nowhere with him and the funny thing is, I really did start to catch some serious feelings for him. He would have been my first if he would have gone all the way that day in his living room. I thought he finally gave in and was about to move our friendship to a relationship of some sort. Didn't happen. The way he was touching all on me and shit you would have thought but, once we reached the couch something changed.

I won't lie my feelings were hurt as no man had ever touched me let alone slept with me, my upbringing didn't allow it. Plus a craving for him had grown inside me.

I would get inside the lives of these individuals I felt

something was there happening far more important than I

knew. I needed to get in and find out I would.

# Taquan

*For Sunday September 11th, 2016*

*"You will be made rich in every way so that you can be generous on every occasion, and through us your generosity will result in thanksgiving to God.*

*2 Corinthians 9:11""*

*"Honor belongs to God and to God alone be the glory. For nothing done is done unto your-self but unto God. For who can get create for creating themselves. As much as obtained riches and wealth give the impression of self-made because of testimony of accomplishing through obstacles. Sorry to have you so missed informed and fooled into believing the total opposite of grace and mercy which abound forever. Predictability is in the prediction made in your life through control given to outer forces. The only honest and true prediction that should be in your life is Gods words for it will surely come to pass. And he predicted letting the wrong outside force conduct situations*

*in your life opens the day for temptation who desire you*

*and who reward is death. He says diligent search for truth*

*for its not far off from you, diligent being an action verb*

*stands out. Watch the thing you take in and make important*

*in yourself, for out of the heart flows the issues in your life.*

*God said continually abound in me when you wake, when*

*you out and about, and when you lay down to sleep at*

*night. Oh you of little faith who deal uncontested with folly*

*which has become a great burden to you and your*

*offspring's. It was said judge not less you be judge but I say*

*to you a discerning heart judges between not people but*

*between whether a thing is good are bad. For this you alto*

*judge so that your soul have peace within you."*

# (Scene 6 That same morning)......

"Morning bruh what we having for breakfast this morning?" Tyrone asked me as he enters my balcony through my office and sat down at the table to join me. I was sitting out on my office balcony, when Tyrone arrived, reading the New York Times which held information no local newspaper would have.

"You late." I said finally glance over at him since he sat down and looked at my watch.

"Had a little unsuspected situation but I'm here now so let's get to it." He said as he reached across the table for a bangle and then some of the bacon out before them. The server came with a tray of beverages and offered him orange juice, tea, or coffee. He accepted a glass of orange juice and a cup of coffee.

"This situation is here for a reason." I said ready to discuss the reason for this early visit It was 8:30 in the morning.

After making love to my wife I wanted to hold her but knew this developing situation needed my attention. If it slipped by me and blow up it could hurt me being nominated to some extent and that couldn't happen. So I continued to tell him my conclusion.

"What's obvious is usually the unobvious in our situation and they moving too obvious especially coming by way of Cuba. These two countries has no ability to negotiate together to create treaties and build trust for better relationship between countries. They continue to want the different worlds who all have agreed to conduct business outside its borders and not within and allowing tourist to visit pacific areas. The state of predicament has been their norm for years with no real perspective of changing as much as they keep changing and negotiating the some business agreements between both countries. There are a few channels this situation with need to be evaluated on before we can actually interfere with our team. So let the process happen, under scrutiny surveillance for this may be bigger than at first glance and we need to be prepared for that by closely watching their moves and actions. Coming from their direction as I read in the reports, was noted on a few occasions in the reports, their crafty and dignified which makes them roofless. Their countries ability to stay independent all these years is their core of strength to feel the need to not answer to anyone else's government." I finished.

"So you believe this could run deep." Tyrone asked me.

"I wouldn't underestimate it. It's hard to tell how deep or what really are there operations even through there is some drug activity. So again make sure this case that's opening for investigation into the operation happening now will give us Intel on who we are dealing with. We really need to identify and name who these individuals are and their role in this operation. Once that happen in the next few week make sure the information is true and accurate comparing your report to the officials report so that we have current and updated information at all times." I replied.

After talking to Tyron about where the presidential nominations campaign was at on our tours and when the votes were scheduled to take place. He left my office and I made a few phone calls to some people I might need to take a trip to Cuba. My brother was overseeing an operation in place that was part of his mission and most people wouldn't find it ethical. Practical it was and being done it had been for years and at times it seemed they took 10 steps forward to take just as many back but a war at this point on drugs wasn't a prospective for war. But, it was and held the wrong people in a position to undermine the laws and demoralize other people lives, destroying families and communities in the process.

Law was such an undefined way to systemize society as a whole because of its simple but complicated diversified conjunction in the worse of situations. To say things was at cut and dry as people were to believe is a total misgiving for Law are subjective to only those within its realm of territory. UN deals with the law that governs agreements between countries, and then you have country laws for people living in a large population. Individuals are then subject to local official's rules and regulations of towns and states of smaller population and based on circumstance of environment. Not including the many local social groups who oppose rules and requirements on its members that if violated could be penalized on under state laws or require state law to defuse.

To fully understand the system and its developments you would have to go back to what the 4 father vision was in the declaration of independence. No time to explain all that for time was of the essence and it's been taught for years. What's more deliberating is the fact that it was all about to come to an end before everyone without no real notice that it has. A decree had been put forth into place a few years back, or should I say centuries back, a group of undisclosed members had come together to develop what was the "Escape plan" for citizens in the day of reckoning. Guarded by guards in an undisclosed location it had been kept in reserves for the two who shall come to receive it as an inheritance. The day came and the two did receive it.

The day my little brother was token from me to live and be subject to the cruelties of the system this law has been implied to. Its implication into place has hurt the major of the people living within its boundaries and beyond. What has been done can't be changed but, I vowed that day to get revenge for my brother. But, upon receiving my decree that only I could have access to by recognition of a mark that resembled a tattoo, was placed on my body. That had be the first time I seen my brother in 15 year I was 3 years older than him. We both seemed to have grown into man but shared so much of the same characteristics. That growing up apart did not damage our relationship we actually seemed stronger, separation usually made the heart grow fonder.

We had to stay a year in that location and study the decree and understand the fundamentals from elders two whom had aided in its publication and therein. We were put through the test of surviving the natural while only living with the natural. They held the fort down and made it home against all odds determined to see the mission through as they as learned and shared each other aspect of the experience living in two different words , as well as, a third life experienced in my earlier years with my parents. And a four is the experience of the life in west bubble, as they had been blind folded when brought there for that life changing experience. We both returned to our prospective live more determined than ever to continue what we had so unwilling be unable to accept till now.

We remained in contract the remainder of the 10 years we had left to complete our full, all levels of education. At no point we're we able to go below a 3.8 average but we both managed to keep 4.0's which wasn't a surprise giving our level of intelligent from birth. We was accepted with open arms by the people we subject our self to in bondage and sacrifice as we both was well financially since birth. This build an appreciation inside them that was beyond expression, there was something to say about the unknown to man.

The time for the world to know what has been transforming before them but was unknown to them was approaching. Do to the transparency of it appearance to appear unrecognizable to those who may desire to understand it, it looked as if nothing exit. Surrounded by only the important elements needed to sustain it in its place for the people to follow it and prosper without the ruling of evil should have had it in the beginning. Combined by the geological studying's from of old with hundreds of years of documentation and bind by elements that doesn't change from day to day, year to year, generation to generation, societies of old to societies of new. None of the founding factors has change human lived off shelter, water, food, and clothing elements of survival from the beginning.

What these profound elements did warrant was protection and in the aspect all was left subject to others who acted as chiefs. Protection of valuables for human's survival had token front center, the cause of actions, some without logic. Uncharacteristic for peaceful living, amongst the Gods who lives here, for their people; sealing, killing, manipulating, degrading, and destroying. No evil deed will be left undone, aborted from the very place it took root and destroyed from the face of the earth. The system will be abolished and it reign shall rain no more, for the leaders of such ruling had strict warning sent to them. And decide continually to be aggressive and their hold on the weak and refusing to retreat. So thing will transpire that their heavy machinery they have prepared in the defense of such coming will trap them off in there death. How arrogant of them to thing building they self-isolation would protect their food, water, clothing, and the things they so cherished. May they evil protect them in their day of wrath as they were so hoping.

I had been seating at my desk making the phone calls to have the new TriO case imposed. I couldn't leave my brother in this situation alone. So I had written off to implement the operation into place and approved the zones with the borough councilors. The operations proved the strategy was fruitful with the seizing of over almost 20 kilos of cocaine moving at an average of 14,000 per kilo removing close to 250,000 off the streets. Untaxed free money it was considered and when token in to custody and processed was then donated to an agency and probably never reaches it intended. That was the highest complains coming in on the city council evaluation records "unfunded" complains from local charities from the city after approval. The system wasn't a legitimate system clarification by it justification had been judged.

# Tyrone (Scene 7 later that night)…………

"Yo fellas what's going on?" I had just got to the pool hall where Tuck and Keith was hanging out at.

The place was lit for a Wednesday night. But that was the norm for this spot here; it had its reputation as being one of the go to spots. With its high celebrity frequency, hottest Dj's mixing, and the latest trendsetters from these new reality shows shit stayed lit around here. I decided it was time to see where Tuck and Keith head was at when it came to what the streets was talking about. Knowing how much they loved the life style of the rich hood life. Flashy women, cars and jewelry turning up in the best of places and getting drunk as fuck was their norm. They didn't only get illegal money. I knew if anything they knew something about something. They loved living this certain street life and was building connects.

Too much drugs has come off the streets in the last year or two, people want to know who getting that sh-money. I was.

"So look who decided to join us. Here go the man himself."

Tuck said.

I took off my suit jacket and hung it up on the hook in the section they were occupying. By the way Tuck was talking I knew he was on his third drink of liquor and by the $4^{th}$ drink, his words will be incomprehensible. Keith on the other hand was skimming the room for a lady to take home and it wasn't to meet mama. I knew I had to meet this visit quick and short and I wanted them to understand the ramifications of their actions and not hold him liable he wouldn't get into all the that tonight as he see he was almost to late but, this was the time to get the juicy gossip, the information he wanted to know. Before I go any further let me introduce who my boys are and how way back we go.

I knew Tuck and Keith since elementary school they stayed in the same neighborhood I foster cared to till I left at 16. Living in the Bedford-Stuyvesant area of Brooklyn on Nostrand Avenue, I had seen and learned about the street live first hand by what was happening in the neighborhood. Africans-American left Harlem in the early 1930's to escape the overpopulation taking effect in and the better housing opportunities in Brooklyn. Bed-Stuyvesant was one of the first free African-American communities in the US. Italians and Jews had previously owned it before African-Americans and Caribbean's started immigration from the south following the great depression. The Brooklyn navy yard was another reason for this large immigration shift as it held employment opportunities.

As they both had lived on the block since birth everyone knew them especially by the age of 6 when I met them. We went to the same elementary school and high school before splitting up right before college. We played sports together when we was younger, went to parties together as we got older, even fucked a few chicks from the same crew. But I had to always keep good grades when no matter work and at time didn't have as much freedom as they did. Tuck mother didn't play and made him go to school even if she had to work him. He got the chicks he was fucking with to do his homework the good grades got him leniency. He didn't mind going to school as that was the place to show off for him his mother brought him whatever he wanted. I think she felt bad about his pops not being around. Keith on the other hand lived with both his parents who never seemed to be around; his grandmother was there most the time but, couldn't tell him what to do. A tragedy happened with his parents after he graduated high school I wasn't sure what as I had already left for college 2 years prior.

Tuck had attended community college and got an Associate degree in Business Management. He landed employment right out of college and been working there ever since. He was now a regional manager for a retail outlet. Keith inherited some money from his parent and started a cleaning business that was doing pretty good. His grandmother had took the younger siblings and moved to the other part of town. Keith had decided to keep the house here and was still living there now. We kept in contract over the years that we separated as we never really did come back together as hang out buddy, do to the difference in our life styles. We were all in our early 30's now and a lot had changed while some shit just reminded the same, my boys hadn't changed. With few real responsibilities, no kids, and no plans on settling down anytime soon playing they were, and apparently not done yet.

"My bad Tuck." I said as I sat down at the table. "I apologize about my demeanor earlier I had a situation at work that was on my mind."

"Oh. That secret job you do for a living and won't tell your boys about. Oh that's the work you referring to huh?" Keith said backing up Tuck and I didn't like the undertone in any of their voice.

"Yea." I said with a matter-of-fact tone. "If you guys got something to say. Say it." I said sitting up straight to look them both in their faces.

"You not a cop now are you Tyron?" Keith asked as he was the oldest of us three and knew he was sometimes in the pass respected as such. The key word was it was in the pass, and even then he had limits. I didn't play with the arrogance in these streets even as a young boy and they knew that. I hope they knew that whatever was about to transpire was at a point of no return.

"A cop." I had to laugh. Only do to my birth right did I even want to affiliate with such tactics the system was made of.

"You ask me that after all these years. After all the work you seen me put in up to this point." I said.

These drugs and money didn't come off these streets easily. They had to back a few niggas down even let off a few rounds. They were bugging right now had they had things all the twisted.

"I think you two needs to choose your words wisely and really think about what you are assuming." I said.

"You didn't answer my question." Keith said rather aggressively. I really wasn't feeling his attitude. I double check to make sure my gun was on me. They tried something stupid they would regret it.

"We just asking you a simple question bruh, you know we supposed to be homeboys but lately we haven't been feeling like your homeboys." Tuck said.

"I don't know what you getting at. We not kids anymore life moves on. If you and you." I said pointing at both of them. "Feel this is the life for you then by all means live it. I don't move like I use to, if you two want to take that as moving suspicious that is on you. But, for the record I'm definitely not a cop I'm in a way, in a higher position then a cop is. That's for sure. That's an insult dwags."

I have seen what cops go through on the streets and at the stations we evaluate them yearly and get reports quarterly, their the less on the professionals levels of the judicial system. They make a lot of mistakes.

"This dude said he higher than a cop. I never knew a drug dealer to be higher than a cop's level in less the feds step in."

"Yoo watch your mouth." I had to look around my surrounding to make sure no lurkers were in the shadows listening.

"Nigga watch what you say to me I'm not going to say it again." I took my gun out and put it on the table. "You never seen me sell a drug a day in my life no matter what connects I had in these streets. You guys picked up and drop off, that's all." I said lowering my voice a bit. "I never asked you to sell anything and you did not have to accept the offer, to join in on the operation. I did business with you two out of our friendship but, never had to. This operation was all mines from my contracts here in the states to my contracts in Cuba. What you don't get is that the whole operation isn't even illegal. Whenever you did do a transaction it's was always set-up at the boarders, with the buyer never even touching American soil, your only connect to the whole operation was me." Dumb fucks. I smell greed I thought to myself. "So again where are the un-neutral feelings coming from?"

"Man the streets are getting hot with a lot of people asking questions we hear they plotting a stick up on us." Tuck said shaking his head. He seems worried and poured himself another cup from the patron bottle on the table.

"What type of questions?" I directed my question to Tuck as Keith had got quiet since my gun hit the table, I didn't care, nor did I appreciate the way he was looking at me. Little did these two know the whole operation with them was over and this was the last time they were to hear from me again. I can't chance their inner ability to complete the mission they was showing strong vulnerability issues, never good for business. I couldn't chance me and my brother positions being compromised one bit. These two had to go before they caused a real problem as it was already brewing.

"Street niggas are saying that the product is being brought but not put on the streets and they're not feeling that. Cops and Detectives has been in the hoods lately asking his any new people been out here"

Sometimes I wondered how they could put with so much of the streets when neither one of them really had to. I felt like there was something they weren't telling me but, for now I would let it go. What's done in the dark does come to light. Whatever it was didn't include me for sure I knew my position and where I stand. They had yet to understand me but will be subject to its warmth if it ever came to that.

"Boy I'm not sure what any of that may mean -." Keith cut me off.

"We think you the reason for this talk in the street."

"And if I am." I said looking at him.

"Then I think you should explain to us what it is we really doing here."

"I don't have to explain nothing we agreed to the terms and condition on the grounds of how we will do business. That is all the conversing about this operation I am doing with you and Tuck."

"So you are not doing no underhanded business and we not knowing about it." Tuck said.

I was done with this conversation which seems to be coming back in full circle about what was missing on the streets.

"Yall talking crazy."

"We talking real." said Keith. "Shit if you got as down but making side money we are losing."

Now this nigga had my attention so money was the issue, the root of all evil. We could have grown up together and been thick as thieves but, there was greed and I was definitely seeing the symptom. Here and now between me and what was supposed to be my homeboys. This chapter I was closing the relationship between us was becoming something totally the opposite of what it had been and I didn't feel responsible for that. My obligation came in knowing what I know now and finishing what I started. Damn man my boys were in the streets and it looks to be deeper than I ever imagined. I put my gun away because they weren't worth, it in this way, perhaps they services can be used in a different way. I stood up grabbed my jacket and walked off without ever looking back, they were playing a dangerous game and may the best man win.

I got in my car and started the engine as I pulled off my brother words came back to me *"Don't mix business and pleasure bruh. If they your boys, like you say they are, don't let them lines cross. Because then you will have to make a tough decision and finish what you started."*

I won't be responsible for what they got themselves into, unless its cover in our agreement which we all had signed copies of. They were actually in violation as nothing I gave them was to ever touch the streets. In the intend it did under subjection to full prosecution of the law, United States. The most important section of the contract was read:

*"the ability given to the highest ranking official declared as highest official by the New York State Supreme Court and can held in custody and detained, without restricts and full liberty to the declared high official, due to suspicious activity. Seemingly to jeopardize or compromise in any form government security, Etc. "*

Fuck a cop I could lock any one of them up at any time without needing a warrant I already had grounds and the contract was in effect. The contract was effective until 1 year after operations held be aborted and officially sealed closed with no further trace to it ever exiting. The money wasn't all was worth it illegally when you getting it legally. They received 50,000 per drop off and did one every 2 to 3 months, they were typically large shipments and took them arranging it for loading at the borders a day in advance. They were paid very well for their services and both held good paying jobs I didn't get it. Tuck was a regional manager position made him almost 70,000 a year before taxes. Keith's cleaning business, plus his inheritance from his parent's death had him living pretty well. Having money definitely wasn't a problem for these dudes greed was and will make the whole situation sick with its bitterness. Greed seats down deep and the heart of him who lets it in and it grows.

I knew, even though that was my last time seeing them; that wasn't their last time seeing me. I pulled out my gun to let these nigga know I wasn't playing and they knew it was more to it then what the eye could see. They had in they eyes the thirst that creep in first as the sign to the first stages of your greed happening.

They wanted my contact it would make them both the man, anybody in the hood that could get to me for it would become that nigga, wasn't happening. Dumb fucks. I was stopping the hood from reaching the major connects that was bringing the drugs in and sending it right back to Cuba and it surrounding territories but, for different reasons it was being used in the US. There was a better resource market that could use the substance then the pleasurably way one was accustomed to using it over the states.

I decided to grab something to eat from the dinner not too far from where I lived. It was1:30 and its usually slow till after 3 when the night spots started closing and 6 am morning rush hour. I pulled into the parking lot and got out. I walked in and the aroma and soft music playing was inviting. I looked around for a seat.

"Hey Tyron see a seat you want?"

"What good Stephanie?" I said to the server/sometimes hostess. She was Hostess tonight I guessed. "Yo put me in that corner over there by the window."

I needed something to occupy my eyes besides the inside of this joint..

"Sure." She said and lead the way.

I followed her over to the table as she put that extra switch in her walk as she did from time to time. She wasn't my type though; I was type picky do to my nature of things not just anybody could be in my life at this point, especially. I really didn't care too much because if that thing my brother constantly talks about isn't there, in his words "you're wasting your time…." I agreed it served me no purpose beyond pleasurable till I found that one. If that was even possible be a minute since I gave a relationship a try but, we won't go there right now. I had to make sure tighter security was on these fuck boys. They bet not have nothing to do with nothing that's my word.

She sat the menu down as I sat down. "Enjoy." She said looking me over before walking away.

I looked at the menu to see if there were any specials. Nothing of real interest to me on there, so I ordered a stake with vegetables and garlic bread with a side salad something not too heavy as late as it was. The waitress came and took my order when she walked away I pulled out my cellphone. 20 minutes into me eating my food which was pretty good the reason he came to this dinner at times. A couple came in and sat in the both in front of mines, I had noticed hem when they got close as my head had been facing down toward my plate. I looked up and caught eye contact with a female who didn't look too happy. Looking at the guy walking behind her confirmed my opinion I started eating a little faster I didn't want to hear this start right now.

"Yo seat on that side."

He said to her pointing to the seat that was in front of me having her back facing me. I glance up at home boy and knew from his eyes on me that his action was because of my presents. He sat down at their table and I continued eating. My phone kept buzzing from notifications and I turned it on silent so I could enjoy my food and it not gets cold.

'I'm tired of your shit Vanessa you always on my back about these hoes man." I heard oh' boy say.

"I'm always on your back about these hoes and everything else you do because you haven't changed much in the last 5 years I've been with you. You make promises after promises but nothing changes."

You can tell from her voice she was trying to talk softly.

Dude didn't care he was looking at his phone when I

looked up.

"Nothing changes bitch your crib got bigger. You don't

have to work if you don't want to and I purposed to you

twice and you said no. What more do your ass want girl?

Most women would be happy with that. I'm just saying."

"What are you just saying? You can do better? The funny

thing is I'm telling you that very same thing but you would

rather it be a different woman you change to then making a

change in your life to keep the woman you got. You so

freaking comfortable with the things you do. Why?" She

asked him.

"Because that me that is how the fuck you met me. Oh now

it's a problem. That's your problem not mines."

My waiter walked over and asked me did I need anything

else I told her no jus the check. The food for the couple

came out and placed on the table I looked over and he was

texting I his phone. I continued minding my business and prepared to leave once I pay my bill.

"You know what I'm out. Find you r own way home." He stood up and threw some money on the table.

"You see your disrespect Jeff. You see how you treat me." She said rising her voice for the first time.

"I treat you how you act. Take your ass to the house and you better be there when I get there." He walked out the door and kept it pushing.

I refused to look up that time and see if that to was directed at me. My waiter walked over and placed a black folder on the table containing my bill. I placed two 20's inside and got up to leave, as I walked pass shorty still seating at the table, I noticed she was crying. I shook my head and decided to go to the rest room before leaving as I had a 30 minute drive home. I walked out the dinner after using the bathroom and a female was standing in front with an umbrella over her head it had begun to rain.

"Ma'am?" It was the hostess who came out behind me.

The female standing in front turned around to the voice of the other female and we locked eyes. Again. It was the female who had been seating with her man at the table in front of me. She turned her glaze to the hostess who had come out behind me. I turned and headed into the parking lot.

"There aren't any available cabs at the moment. Sorry." Stephanie said apologetically.

"Is there a bus stop nearby?"

"Girl where you from?" Stephanie started laughing and the voices became too distance for me to hear. I heard enough to know what had happened and why she was stranded. I got in my car and started the engine. The bus stopped working here at 11. Which made me wonder the same things "where was she from"?" I pulled out the parking lot to her trying to make a phone call the rain had begun to pick up a bit. I got out the car and walked over to her.

"Hey. I'm Tyron." I said. She looked at me looking more hurt than ever. For some reason it bothered me.

"If you don't mind I could give you a ride." I watched her as she hesitated for a few second to think it through.

I put my hands in my pocket and hopped this chick understood I was getting wet.

"I'm Vanessa. Thank you and I would appreciate that." She finally said and walked towards my car.

We walked the short distance to my car parked in the street in front of the dinner. I opened the car door for her. When she was seated I walked around to the driver side and got in. I turned the heat on low to warm her up from being in the rain.

"Thank you." she said and gave me her address to put in the GPS system.

I pulled off and the waft of her perfume in the car was enticing. I turned some music on from the car Bluetooth from my phone. Filling the car with J. Cole's music. Something to take my mind off her, the female I didn't know anything about, seating next to me. Her hand reached over and turned the music down.

"Who are you?"

That shit caught me off guard. "Tyron why what's up." I glanced at her then back to the road.

"I'm interested in knowing how a man as young looking and as…" she stop took a deep breath and picked up somewhere else. "Instead of just rolling down your window and yelling shorty you need a ride. Get in. You got out your car, in the rain. You introduced yourself to me and seemed patient with me and then you opened my car door for me. My man doesn't even open the car door for me. I can't remember a time he did."

Shit. I didn't know what to say, everybody was different, raised different for that matter. I didn't want to offend shorty but he was right, she accepted that from man. She has to change what she allowed from the man she got involved with. I decided to play it safe with my advisement. I liked something about her that made we want to tell her.

"I was raised with manners that made everlasting impressions on me." I gave her one of my smirks.

"See what I'm saying who are you? Men don't talk like that these day all articulate like that. They speak simple and their manners are simple doesn't go beyond the usual politeness."

I didn't know what she wanted me to say about that that was her opinion. I had a better question

"Where you from that you thought buses would be running so late?" I asked.

"I am from here I had just lost track of the time and didn't realize it was so late. The dude I was just with had a little more in his quality when we first meet. It is part of the reason I liked him and agreed to a date with him. He had a nice charisma. What I didn't know was how friendly he was with that charisma with other females till a year into the relationship females would pop up with all sort of drama. He promised me he would change the first time few times and did for a while. But, that only lasted a short period as the next rumor and round of drama I was hearing is he may have a kid on the way. This was a few months ago and the reason I am so pissed now. I feel like he isn't being honest about the situation with me. That was actually the stir for me sweetie." She said then got a little quiet. I looked over at her and she seemed deep in thought. I turned back around.

"But, then that controlling male nature came out and he now threats me with if I leave him this will happen or that. I pay it no mind and I'm just counting the days till I meet my goal and disappear on his ass. I won't fight him, nor am I sacred of him, nor will I pull my family into the situation unless it calls for that on its own and so far it hasn't. But I got myself into this relationship and I will get myself out. He can sleep if he wants but every dog has its day. She leaned back in the chair seeming happy to have gotten that off her chest.

"I'm sorry for talking so much I needed to get that off my cheat as I don't talk to much people within my circle because I don't want them asking questions and mending in our business about what he do. There could be some real repercussions. People don't tell you everything coming in somethings you have to find out on your own and mama always said "when a person show you who they are you should believe them."

"You good. I agree with a lot of what you said. You seem to have a clear head despite the circumstance. That's being level headed and seems to work in people favor."

"Omg. I can just seat and talk to you for hours. Who are you Tyron you feel so familiar to me."

I gave shorty a puzzled look and I don't remember meting her if I did.

"The house on the right the blue one right there." She said pointing to her crib.

"Nice neighborhood." I said.

"Yea pretty decent neighborhood I grew up not too far from here. Where's your cell phone?"

"I reached in my pocket and pulled it out. she took it from my hands and then asked me the password. I pressed it in she entered her name and number. Yea I was satisfied with that. She passed me back my phone after calling her phone from my phone. I will give you a special ring tone you seem special and rare. Have a safe trip home and I couldn't thank you enough." She said as she got out.

'Not a problem beautiful. Speak to you soon." I said.

"I hope you mean that as I'm looking forward to hearing from you." She smiled closing the door and walked to her door and let herself in. She waved bye before closing her crib door behind her.

I looked in my review at the car that had been following us and knew that she would need to hear from me sooner rather than later. Her man was on a violent mission who could be dangerous for her no matter her braveness to want to handle the situation herself, at times you need help with problems bigger then you can handle. I pulled off heading home that car wouldn't make it anywhere now the primer of my residents. Matter of facts the question would start as soon as I pulled off with some guys that wouldn't hesitate in killing him if he made the

wrong move. I would definitely be back around Vanessa.

# Sara (Scene 8 One month later)…………..

I haven't been feeling too well lately and made an appointment to see my doctor. I asked Taquan to go with me and he said he would but at 1 o'clock he called me and said he would meet me at the doctor's office he was tied up with something. The appointment was for 2:30 so I said fine. I had been at Lil Jones Village" a further distance from the doctor's office then my home. I was expecting him to be there when I got there as I was nervous for some reason. When I got there I signed in and took a seat and filled out the paperwork, after handing it back to the receptionist. I pulled out my phone and text him because he damn sure wasn't here. Before I could put my phone back in my bag from texting him he walked in the door.

Damn this man was fine as hell I was blessed to be his wife. My husband stood near 6ft off by 2inches slender and athletically built. He had a dark caramel complexion that felt as smooth as it looked. His dark hair feature brings out his face giving him an exotic male look. From deep in his heritage roots he was a fair skinned America Negro. A gorgeous one, might I add. He possessed so much man power it radiated off of him when you was in his present. Up against the best of them I witnessed my husband hold his own. I had appeared at some of his campus rallies he participated in during college days and witnessed how he wins over an audience with standing ovation. He caught the attention of many who couldn't resist the truth in his words pertaining to social and economic political problems. And the tone in which he delivered it held the determination everyone respected in a leader. Someone who believed in what it is they was presenting and strongly represented that cause. He volunteered a lot in the communities in the in cities of different states.

Taquan had a promising future and everyone knew it even back then he was destined for greatness. He was the true definition of an all-America boy regardless of the color of his skin. As I have grown up around mostly privilege kids all my life I had learn their concepts early in my life. I knew I wasn't and never would be are fit into their particular world. I went to school with them, mingled with them at social events, and whatever else us socialites do in representation of our status quo. I remember asking ma' ma when I was a little girl why we had to go to places like this and not just stay home and hang with the other people like us that we knew. We had plenty of friends who lived and looked like us but didn't act snobby like them elected socialites.

I was 9 at the time and didn't know that what truly separated social status was your money worth. Mama did tell me that she said that when you are invited to the king table you go. In doing so, you get both, God's blessing and men's blessing upon you. I didn't understand anything mama said and was even more confused than I was previously. I kept the concern in my heart but church life was dominant in my family and we want every Sunday to our Baptist church. That's where I began to understand mama talk and parables she loved throwing around and it humbled my spirit to indifference, while being reserved. In servicing others you in turn are serviced. Sitting at the king's table we were serviced like him in royal, God's appreciation for our honorable service in contentment to higher authority. I understood and silently prayed I let go of all resentment I hoovered deep in my heart.

I continued to engage in the social group I had grew accustom to. In a way I'm happy I did are I would not have met the man of my dreams. For in that social environment I met the man of my dreams. He was being adored and seemly praised by others by his astonishing words and noble actions. I called it love at first sight "true soul mates." An annual fundraising event had come up where anyone that was someone in our would be attending. At this event there were a few candidates that were up for an all exclusive scholarship to three of the tops schools in the states. The foundation gives out only 3 every 5 year due to the large sum need to cover the cost for the three scholarship packages. It was my first year in grad school and I wasn't going to attend but some of my fret sisters thought it was a great idea and can generally help my future in establishing my own organization. I remembered hating the way the word minority was being thrown around like if not to matter and made less than sufficient. Not even sometimes, by any means of their own, was the cruelty being done deserving.

At this fund raiser is where I met Taquan. I say it was faith because of how many people was at this event, 12,000, and I still managed to meet him. I remembered it like it was yesterday me walking into the venue and looking around at the decor which was always the main exhibit with a fundraiser it spoke of the foundations status quo. How much the people involved really showed by what they put out for the people to see. A shabby fundraiser means you didn't have the proper connects and was raising capital for your cause as suspected. Having an elegant event with all the right people and right décor and commodities would have donation pouring in before the event was over. As the event came to an end and a few of us volunteered to stay behind to help straighten up, I noticed the girls talking about something over in a corner. I walked over to see what I had been missing. A girl name Brittany filled me in.

"Hey Ladies. What's going on what yall being so secretive about?"

"Shhhh." A few of the girls said out of the 5 of them standing there.

"The next up and coming political leader everyone has been talking about is here. He is young and gorgeous looks nothing like a political leader I have ever seen." She said getting giggles from the other ladies.

"Right girl." One of the girls said confirming it for them all.

"So where this mysterious guy yall have been referring to." I said a little jokingly I couldn't believe they was this excited over him.

"Standing right over there." Brittany said pointing.

My eyes followed in the direction she was pointing in. Damn. That man was gorgeous and the smile on his face made it no better. And the company around him wasn't small Politian's. As she dealt with them over the years due to her father serving as DEA for the criminal justice system at one point in his career. The chuckling behind me probably because of my own admiration for the man was showing. The chuckling I guess caught his attention because he looking in our direction. For same awkward reason I felt if I moved he would recognized me, and I didn't want him to. I would have rather I be a butterfly on a wall and watched him from afar then he noticing me. Noticing me he did.

When his eye landed on me it's like I felt it and I felt compelled to return the stir. We locked eyes and a smile returned to his face as he nodded and looked away. I turned around to the ladies standing behind me waving. "I told you Brittany." That she did but she couldn't prepare me for the strong way in which I reacted to him. I walked off and started picking up more of the items disregarded by their guess. Something had just happened and I knew my life wouldn't ever be the same for some reason. One look had unraveled me and I had been hypnotized by a man I loved since the day I laid eyes on him.

I looked up at him as he got closer and seen an intents look in his eyes, he didn't look like he had aged at all, since we. He kissed me on my lips before sitting down. I looked passed him at a seen that caught my eye once he came inside the doc office. A man in an all-black suit walked in behind him looking around then walking back outside where another guy I all black was standing. They stood on both sides of the door. This shit was getting weirder by the second. What the fuck was going on with him and what wasn't he telling me. He must of had noticed me looking at the situation perplexed, as when I looked at him, he was looking at me. I looked deep into his eyes to see if I could get a grimace of something there. Nothing. "Taquan. What's—"

"Mrs. Jones."

"Yes." I said looking away from him to the nurse who had called my name. I stood up and walked towards her and felt his eyes pouring into my back. The door closed slowly as I walked in wondering why he didn't come in with me.

The nurse who had called my name walked me into a room gave me one of those piss cups and told me to go into the bathroom over in the corner of the room. To first wipe with an alcohol wipe she gave me in one of those small packages to afterwards wait here in the room. I went into the bathroom and did as she had asked. When I came back out another nurse who was older was in the room typing on a computer. "Hello." I side taking a seat in the waiting chair not far from the desk she was sitting at.

"Hello. Mrs. Sara Jones." She asked looking at me over the rim of her glasses.

"Yes."

"What's your birthday sweetie?"

"9-24-1981." I said hadn't really said my age in a while.

"I'm Ms. Davis the nurse. I will ask you a few questions, weigh you and take you r vitals before you see the doctor. At anything you can ask me anything you need to."

"O.K"

Ms. Davis took the urine I had in a napkin in my hand and placed it on a table. The first nurse who held called my name came in and organized some items on the count to the urine removed a few drops and added them to another medical object. I felt my hands get sweaty I had never been pregnant a day in my life it was frighten and excited at the same time. Ms. Davis weighed me and took my vitals, I was 5'6 weighing 148 pounds and my vitals were fine. She asked me questions like did I smoke, had I ever been to pregnant before, when was my last blood work/doc visit/gyn things of that nature. Once she finished she explained doctor green would be with me shortly to share the results and if needed to she may see me on my way out for any follow-up appt. I politely thanked her and asked her to send that husband of mines in to hear these results with me. She assured me she will and left me alone

to anticipate in my head if I was pregnant or not. A few

seconds later Taquan walked in looking as good as ever a

man looking as good as him you don't grown used to. I

licked my lips and watched his eyes get lusty watching my

movement I smirked and so did he. The doctor entered

behind him clearing his.

"Good afternoon."

"Good afternoon." We said in union.


*To be continued*.............................................

# *Closing* ..........................................................

*Exodus (Chapter) 4 (verse) 1*

*Then Moses said "But suppose they will not believe me or listen to my voice; suppose they say "the lord has not appeared to you."*

*Moses asked God this the day he visited him and told him the people cry has come before him. And "His People" (God said that in the redeeming of an oath to Abraham, Isaac, and Jacob) suffering will now end for them and he will bring them out of Egypt with a mighty hand with a land flowing with milk and honey. Now must people rationality it's where it auto be gearing it in that direction is a hard task that will be filled the usual blood sweat and tears. The Lord God would let the suffering happen longer than necessary for he is of grace and gentle in heart. He has equipped you with the ability to overcome all evil and live peacefully your days without fear. The abilities with in your capabilities are what we the angels the helpers of God have bestowed upon you since youth. Your ancestors are of old and the children to follow will see the face of him whose name is "I AM."*

# Coming Soon………..

**When God Say Yes**

**Episode 2 of 12**

**Novel: Just Read: There is always a story.**

**Release Dates: October & November of 2016**

**Also look for titles:**

**Diversified 4 (Book series) Episode 1**

Made in the USA
Coppell, TX
09 March 2021

51495558R00075